Machines at Work

Machines at the Airport

Siân Smith

Raintree is an imprint of Capstone Global Library Limited, a company incorporated in England and Wales having its registered office at 7 Pilgrim Street, London, EC4V 6LB – Registered company number: 6695582

To contact Raintree:
Phone: 0845 6044371
Fax: + 44 (0) 1865 312263
Email: myorders@raintreepublishers.co.uk
Outside the UK please telephone +44 1865 312262.

Text © Capstone Global Library Limited 2014
First published in hardback in 2014
The moral rights of the proprietor have been asserted.

Edited by Dan Nunn and John-Paul Wilkins
Designed by Cynthia Akiyoshi
Picture research by Elizabeth Alexander
Production by Sophia Argyris
Originated by Capstone Global Library Ltd
Printed and bound in China by Leo Paper Products Ltd

ISBN 978 1 406 25936 0
17 16 15 14 13
10 9 8 7 6 5 4 3 2 1

British Library Cataloguing in Publication Data
Smith, Siân.
Machines at the airport. – (Machines at work)
387.7'36'0284-dc23
A full catalogue record for this book is available from the British Library.

Acknowledgements
We would like to thank the following for permission to reproduce photographs: Alamy pp. 4 (© Steve Vidler), 5 (© ITAR-TASS Photo Agency), 9 (© Kevpix), 12 (© ROUSSEL BERNARD), 15 (© Tips Images / Tips Italia Srl a socio unico), 18 (© imagebroker), 19 (© Richard Wareham Fotografie), 22 (© Jim West); BULMOR Airground Technologies GmbH p. 13; Corbis pp. 7 (© Angelika Warmuth/dpa), 17 (© Patrice Latron); Getty Images pp. 6, 8 (Baerbel Schmidt/Stone+), 10, 23 conveyor belt (Erik Dreyer/Stone); Shutterstock pp. 14, title page (© Robert Cumming), 16, 23 tug (© Thomas Nord), 21, 23 pilot (© Andresr), 23 scanner (© Voznikevich Konstantin), 23 fuel (© Concept Photo), 23 X-ray (© Kasza), 23 radar (© Gertan), SuperStock pp. 11 (© imagebroker.net), 20 (© Ton Koene / age footstock).

Design element photographs of aeroplane (© oriontrail), airport runway (© Cindy Hughes), car engine part (© fuyu liu), and gear cog (© Leremy) reproduced with permission of Shutterstock.

Front cover photograph of an aeroplane reproduced with permission of Getty Images (Yuji Kotani/Taxi Japan). Back cover photograph of an air traffic controller holding light wands (© Andresr) and a tug (© Thomas Nord) reproduced with permission of Shutterstock.

We would like to thank Dee Reid and Marla Conn for their invaluable help in the preparation of this book.

Every effort has been made to contact copyright holders of material reproduced in this book. Any omissions will be rectified in subsequent printings if notice is given to the publisher.

All the Internet addresses (URLs) given in this book were valid at the time of going to press. However, due to the dynamic nature of the Internet, some addresses may have changed, or sites may have changed or ceased to exist since publication. While the author and publisher regret any inconvenience this may cause readers, no responsibility for any such changes can be accepted by either the author or the publisher.

Contents

Some words are shown in bold, **like this**. You can
find out what they mean by looking in the glossary.

Why do we have machines at an airport?

People make machines to do different jobs.

An aeroplane is a machine that helps us to travel to places that are far away.

People go to airports so that they can travel on aeroplanes.

Some machines at airports help people to get their bags onto aeroplanes.

Can a machine spot dangerous things?

People are not allowed to take things onto aeroplanes that could hurt other people.

Metal detectors are machines that can tell if people are carrying guns, knives, or other metal objects.

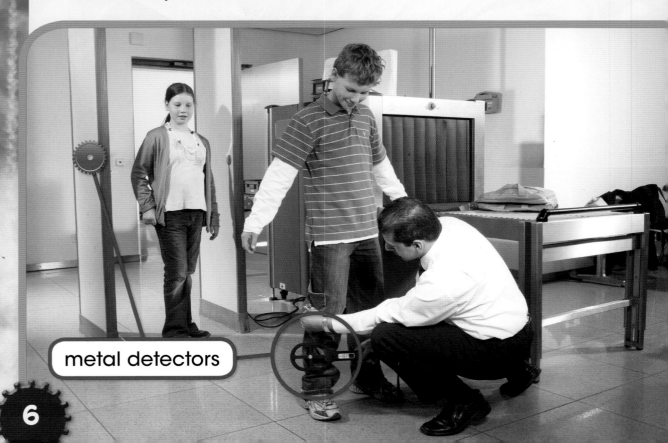

metal detectors

Some machines can take pictures of people that look a bit like an **X-ray**.

They can show if people have hidden things under their clothes.

Every bag at an airport has to go through an **X-ray** machine.

X-ray machines show pictures of things inside a bag, even when it is closed.

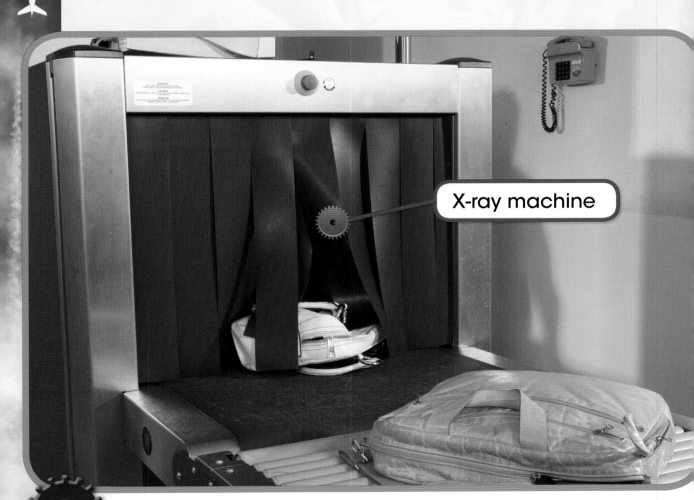

X-ray machine

Different colours show what things are made of.

Airport workers check to see if the pictures show anything dangerous.

How can machines help to move bags?

Each bag is given a number. Computers and **scanners** use the number to tell where each bag is and where it needs to go.

Moving belts called **conveyor belts** and carts carry the bags around.

conveyor belt

conveyor belt

belt loader

Sorting machines stop the bags from getting lost or stuck.

Special machines called belt loaders move bags onto the aeroplanes.

How can machines help to move people?

The doors on an aeroplane are high above the ground.

A giant staircase on wheels helps people to get on and off an aeroplane.

ambulift

If people cannot walk, small buggies can help them to move around an airport.

A machine called an ambulift can lift them up into an aeroplane.

What are the biggest machines at an airport?

The biggest machines at an airport are the aeroplanes.

Jet aeroplanes can carry hundreds of people.

Inside an aeroplane, there are many small machines that help the **pilot**.

Machines show the pilot how fast the plane is going, where the plane is, and how high it is in the air.

What other machines help aeroplanes?

Aeroplanes use their engines to move forward, but most cannot go backwards.

An aeroplane tractor or **tug** moves an aeroplane to where it needs to be.

tug

refueller truck

hose

Aeroplanes are too big to go to petrol stations, but they need **fuel** to make them move.

Refueller trucks with long hoses give aeroplanes the fuel they need.

Which machines help aeroplanes in the ice and snow?

Aeroplanes need to go fast down a runway before they can take off into the air.

Snow ploughs push snow off runways so that planes can take off.

snow plough

runway

de-icer machine

Some parts of an aeroplane stop working if they are covered in ice.

De-icer machines lift airport workers up so they can spray special liquid to melt the ice.

What stops aeroplanes crashing into each other?

Airport workers guide planes around airports, so that they do not crash into each other.

Pictures from **radars** show them any planes in the sky and where they are going.

radar picture

light wand

Airport workers tell **pilots** when it is safe to land by using radios.

They also use light wands to tell pilots what to do when they are on the ground.

What does this machine do?

Can you guess what this airport machine does?

Find the answer on page 24.

26699

NORTHWEST

Picture glossary

 **conveyor belt** moving belt that carries things along

 **scanner** machine that reads information from a label

 **fuel** liquid we put into aeroplanes to make them move

 **tug** type of tractor that pulls things along

 **pilot** driver of an aeroplane

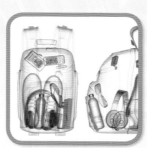 **X-ray** photo that shows the inside of something

 **radar** machine that can tell where aeroplanes are in the sky and which direction they are moving in

Find out more

Books

A Day at the Airport (Time Goes By), Sarah Harrison (Millbrook Press, 2009)

Working at the Airport (21st Century Junior Library: Careers), Katie Marsico (Cherry Lake Pub., 2009)

Website

www.funkidslive.com/features/the-airport
Find out all about airports.

Index

The airport machine on page 22 is a water truck. It collects waste from the toilets of the aeroplane.

Dear Reader,

Most children don't have to stay in hospital for a long time but many do. If you are one of the children who does have to visit the hospital regularly, and maybe even stay over sometimes, you know how tough and lonely that can be. Remember, you don't have to be tough or lonely all the time, you can share your stories with family and friends and ask them to come and visit. Or maybe you can play your own version of the Cloud Babies game together to get you through a rainy day.

If you are lucky enough to be strong and healthy, then perhaps you could make the time in your day to be especially kind and understanding to any children in your school who are spending a lot of time in hospital or who have just returned from a long stay. Ask them to tell you about it. See what games they play on the children's ward. Lend them books for their hospital sleepovers. Send them get well soon cards, and make sure to tell them that they will always belong in school. It will only take a few minutes, but it will make them feel so much happier and, believe it or not, it will make you feel happy too.

Eoin Colfer

All the children's pictures in this book were painted by Juno and Joey Judge.

For the staff of LauraLynn Children's Hospice, who make magic inside its walls – E.C.

For all the Staff in St Johns' Ward, Crumlin Hospital – C.J.

First published 2022 by Walker Books Ltd, 87 Vauxhall Walk, London SE11 5HJ • Text © 2022 Eoin Colfer • Illustrations © 2022 Chris Judge • The right of Eoin Colfer and Chris Judge to be identified as author and illustrator of this work has been asserted in accordance with the Copyright, Designs and Patents Act 1988 • This book has been typeset in Bauer Grotesk OT • Printed in China • British Library Cataloguing in Publication Data: a catalogue record for this book is available from the British Library • ISBN 978-1-5295-0267-1 • www.walker.co.uk • 10 9 8 7 6 5 4 3 2 1

CLOUD BABIES

Eoin Colfer & Chris Judge

WALKER BOOKS
AND SUBSIDIARIES

LONDON · BOSTON · SYDNEY · AUCKLAND

Erin's very first word was CAT.
"Did you say 'cat', honey?" said Dad.
"I don't see a cat."

But then Dad looked up and he saw it, too – a CAT!
"Your very own cloud baby," said Dad.

From then on, Erin was always looking towards the sky, searching for her cloud babies. "It's a snappy-happy crocodile!" she would shout.

"It's a naughty cat!" said Lucy, joining in.

Erin found all kinds of marvellous
and wondrous cloud babies:

A dragon who had
run out of puff,

a fox who was
late for school

and a polar bear
who made snowballs.

One day, Erin felt unwell. She didn't look to the sky, not once.
She'd been poorly before ... but this felt more serious.

Mum and Dad were worried.

Erin would need to spend some time in the children's hospital.

The children's ward was a whole new world,
with beds that buzzed and machines that beeped.

Everyone made Erin
feel welcome and safe.

She even made eleven new
friends on her first day.

Best of all, Erin had her very own team to look after her:

A doctor called Bernadette, who loved ballroom dancing,

Albert, who delivered her extra special meals and was also the hospital DJ,

and lots of wonderful nurses, including Sarika who gave out sparkly unicorn stickers.

While in hospital, Erin always played cloud babies with her dad.
"Look, everyone! It's two dogs swimming!"

And whenever Dad couldn't be there next to her, they still found ways to play.

To be together, all they had to do was ... look up.

Erin was in hospital for a long time.

She missed six turns at taking Florence the class gerbil home.

(Though, Mum really didn't mind because Florence pooped a lot.)

Then one day Dr Bernadette told Erin that while there would still be "hospital days", she didn't have to stay in the hospital any more. Erin was well enough to finally go home.

Erin was excited about going back to school.
But she was also a little nervous.

Everyone had grown so tall.
She had only grown half an inch.

When her teacher, Ms Rose, asked Erin to share a story
about the hospital, she told the class about her cloud babies –
the fox who was late for school and the dragon with no puff.

"Cloud babies are magical," said Erin. "They make people feel better."

Erin thought they would all spot cloud babies together, but instead Ms Rose told the class how clouds were formed. She talked about water vapour and liquid water droplets, and Erin's story really didn't feel so magical any more.

On the way home that day, Erin was quiet.
"Maybe cloud babies are for little kids," she said, finally.

"And I'm in big school now. Can I get a skateboard? Kwame has one."

"And I need to read more science and nature books."

Erin noticed a difference between
her hospital friends and her school friends.

On her hospital days, everyone played together, both big
and little kids; it didn't matter what age you were.

But it wasn't like that in school.

Everyone was six.

And so, Erin decided that she would concentrate on *being* six, too.

And that six-year-olds would not play cloud babies, even on hospital days.

Soon, Erin didn't talk about her cloud babies.
And she did her best not to see them.
That was "kids' stuff".
It was easier to keep her two worlds apart –
hospital and school.

Erin missed her school friends on hospital days.
And she missed her hospital friends, the nurses,
and Albert on school days.

Erin felt like she wasn't fully a part of either group,
like she was floating somewhere in between.
And it didn't feel good.

"I know it's tough," said Dad. "Maybe you could try to find your magical cloud babies again? They always make you, and me, feel better. Maybe you'll see your old friend Dragon again?"

"I don't like cloud babies any more," said Erin.
"Lucy has her ears pierced."

It was so hard to not see the cloud babies in the sky outside the window, to not look up and find ... her friends.

She missed them.

"Sometimes I feel like ... my friends are growing up in real life while I'm here," Erin said to her mum.

"I know. But life goes on in hospital, too," said Mum. "It's a real, warm, loving, important life, that most of your classmates will never see."

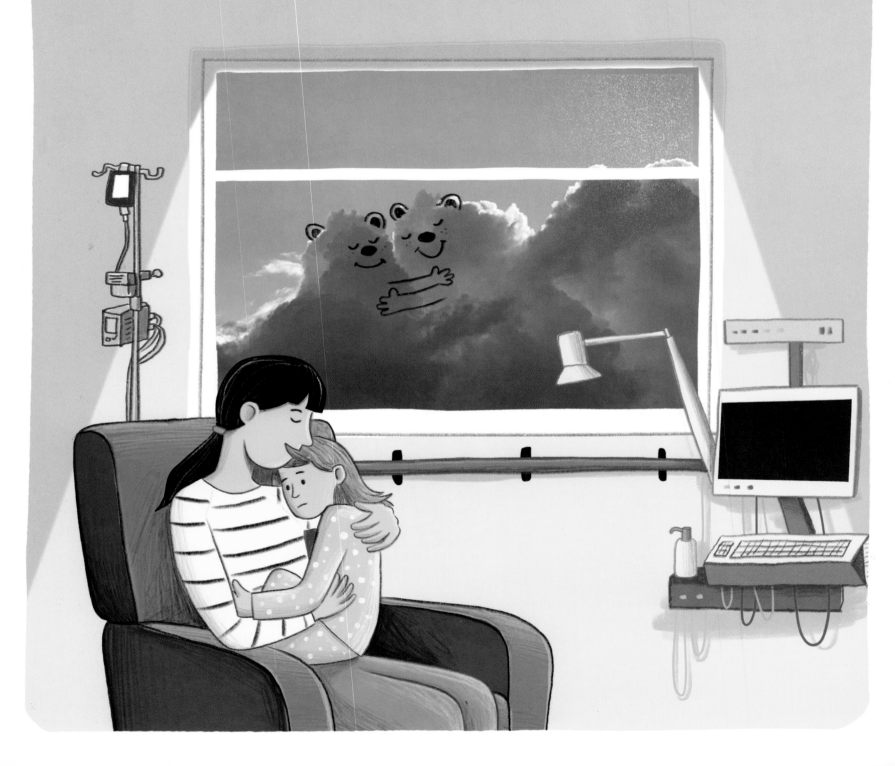

Mum and Dad never gave up on Erin's cloud babies.

They never stopped hoping that Erin would find them again.

The family needed them.

And then Mum saw one cloud baby going

to visit another, and it gave her an idea.

Maybe Erin's friends *could* understand hospital life...

Erin's parents talked to Ms Rose and, together, they made a plan.
Ms Rose was excited to help Erin.

"We have been invited to be Book Buddies
in the children's ward! I hope you've all got your books?
We're going to need our imaginations today!"

At the hospital, Erin showed her teacher and her friends how to play the cloud game. And they finally understood.

"You were completely right, Erin," said Ms Rose.
"Cloud babies *do* make you feel better. They *are* magical."
Erin was happy to see *all* her friends playing the cloud babies game.

"Sometimes, when you're down," said Erin,
"all you need to do is look up."